EXPLORING SPACE

THE SOLAR SYSTEM

WRITTEN BY E.C. ANDREWS

Gareth Stevens PUBLISHING

Please visit our website, www.garethstevens.com. For a free color catalog of all our high-quality books, call toll free 1-800-542-2595 or fax 1-877-542-2596.

Published in 2025 by
Gareth Stevens Publishing
2544 Clinton St.
Buffalo, NY 14224

Written by:
E.C. Andrews

Edited by:
Noah Leatherland

Designed by:
Ker Ker Lee

Cataloging-in-Publication Data

Names: Andrews, E.C..
Title: The solar system / E.C. Andrews.
Description: Buffalo, NY : Gareth Stevens Publishing, 2025. | Series: Exploring space | Includes glossary and index.
Identifiers: ISBN 9781482468694 (pbk.) | ISBN 9781482468700 (library bound) | ISBN 9781482468717 (ebook)
Subjects: LCSH: Solar system--Juvenile literature.
Classification: LCC QB501.3 A537 2025 | DDC 523.2--dc23

This edition is published by arrangement with Booklife Publishing

Printed in the United States of America

CPSIA compliance information: Batch #CW25GS: For further information contact Gareth Stevens at 1-800-542-2595.

Find us on

Photo Credits – Images are courtesy of Shutterstock.com. With thanks to Getty Images, Thinkstock Photo and iStockphoto.

Recurring images – Vector Tradition. Cover – Vadim Sadovski. 2–3 – traXX. 4–5 – 24K-Production, Withan Tor. 6–7 – IvaFoto. 8–9 – FlashMovie, Vadim Sadovski. 10–11 – Aphelleon, Nazarii_Neshcherenskyi. 12–13 – JorisvS, CC BY-SA 3.0 <https://creativecommons.org/licenses/by-sa/3.0>, via Wikimedia Commons, 24K-Production. 14–15 – worldswildlifewonders, Vadim Sadovski, 24K-Production. 16–17 – Vadim Sadovski, Belish, Triff. 18–19 – buradaki, Daniil Disa, Triff. 20–21 – Dima Zel, Andrey Armiagov. 22–23 – NASA images, Sergey Nivens.

CONTENTS

Words that look like <u>this</u> can be found in the glossary on page 24.

WHAT IS SPACE?

Space is the area outside Earth. Many scientists think space may be infinite. This means it goes on forever. However, nobody knows for sure. There is no oxygen in space.

Oxygen is a gas that livings things need to survive. There is no life outside of Earth that we know of. However, many other fascinating things can be found in our solar system.

WHAT IS THE SOLAR SYSTEM?

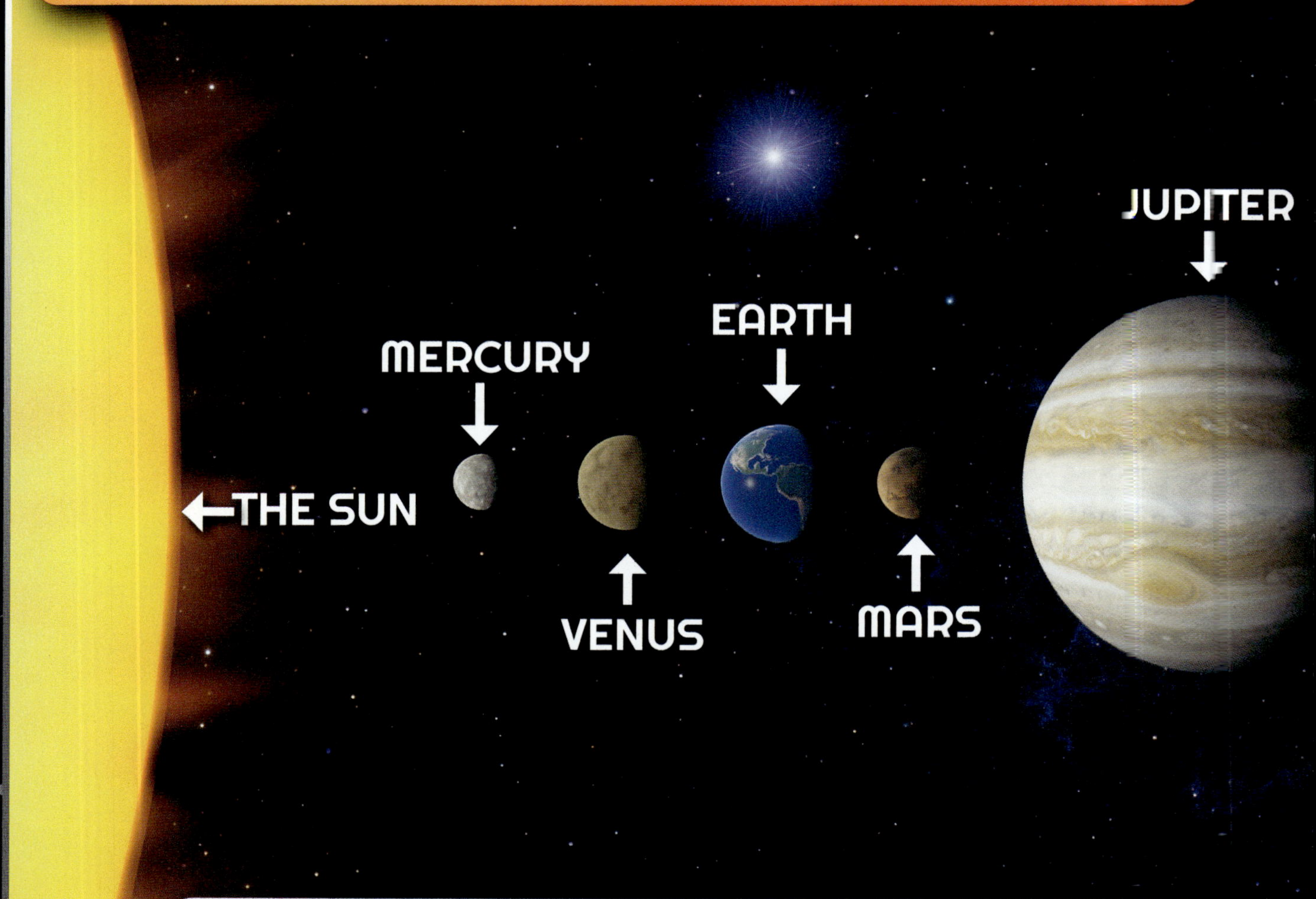

Our solar system is a collection of planets and other objects that orbit around a star we call the sun. The sun is the only star in our solar system. It holds the solar system together

Our solar system has eight planets in it, as well as five dwarf planets. Dwarf planets are smaller than regular planets. Our solar system is also full of comets and asteroids.

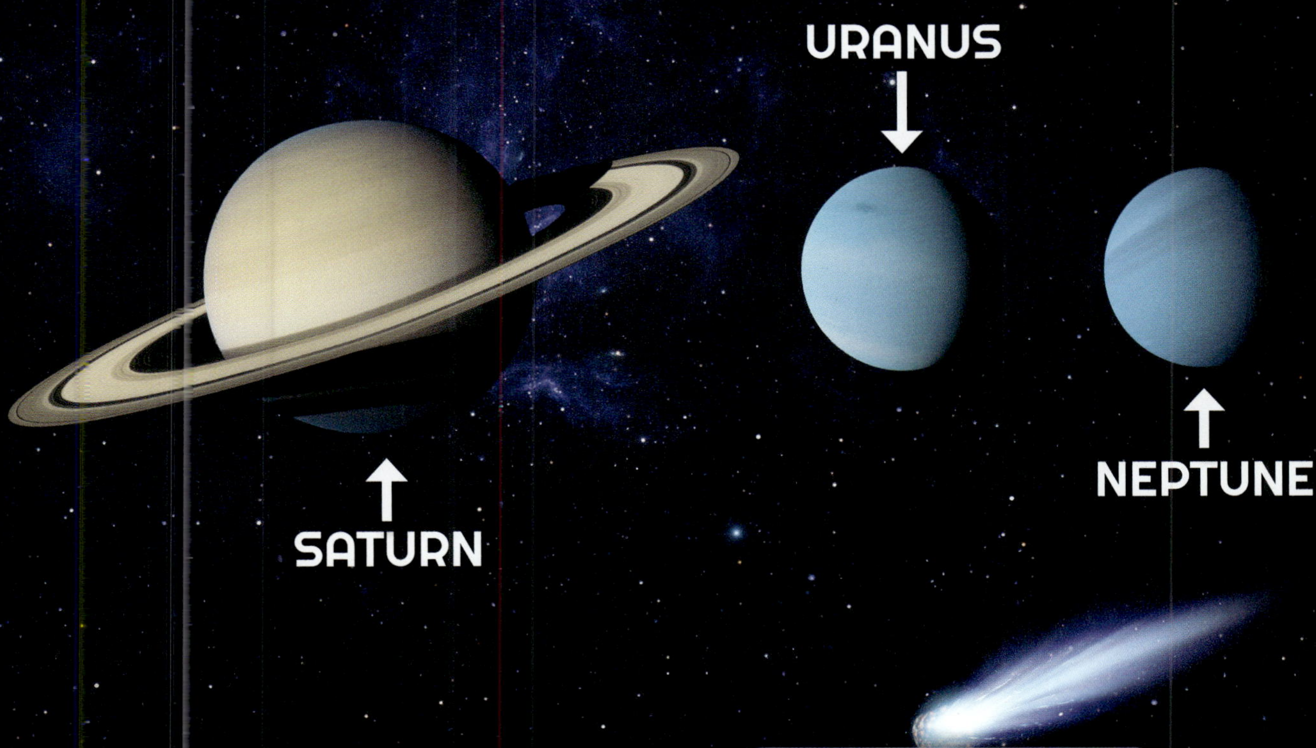

Turn to page 16 to learn more about asteroids!

HOW WAS THE

SOLAR SYSTEM CREATED?

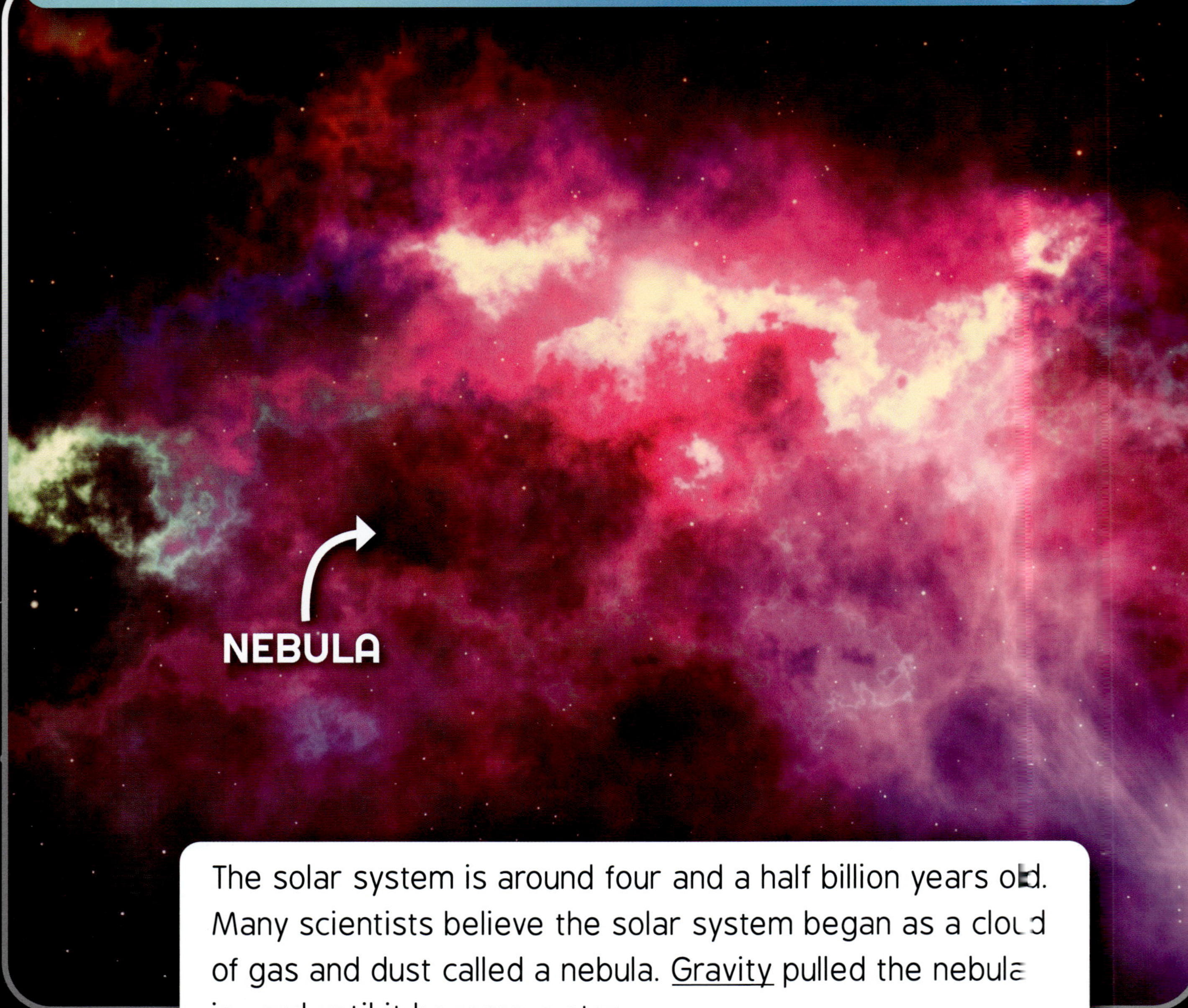

The solar system is around four and a half billion years old. Many scientists believe the solar system began as a cloud of gas and dust called a nebula. Gravity pulled the nebula inward until it became a star.

This star is our sun. The sun's gravity started to pull other things toward it, such as rocks. As this happened, pieces of rock smashed into each other. This created planets.

ORBITS

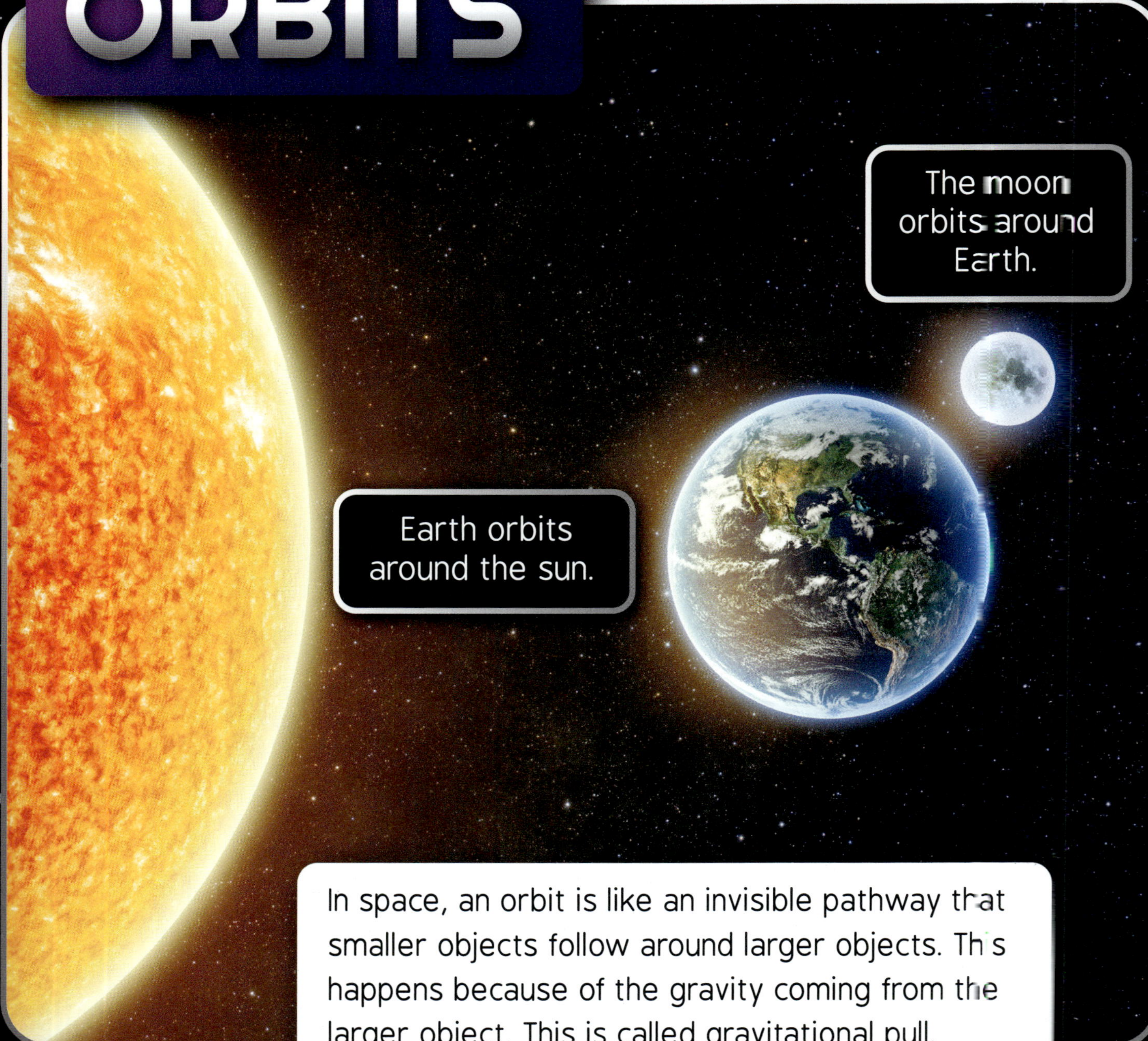

In space, an orbit is like an invisible pathway that smaller objects follow around larger objects. This happens because of the gravity coming from the larger object. This is called gravitational pull.

As planets were created and the sun pulled them in, the weight of the planets began pulling them the other way. This tug-of-war between forces locked the planets in constant orbits around the sun.

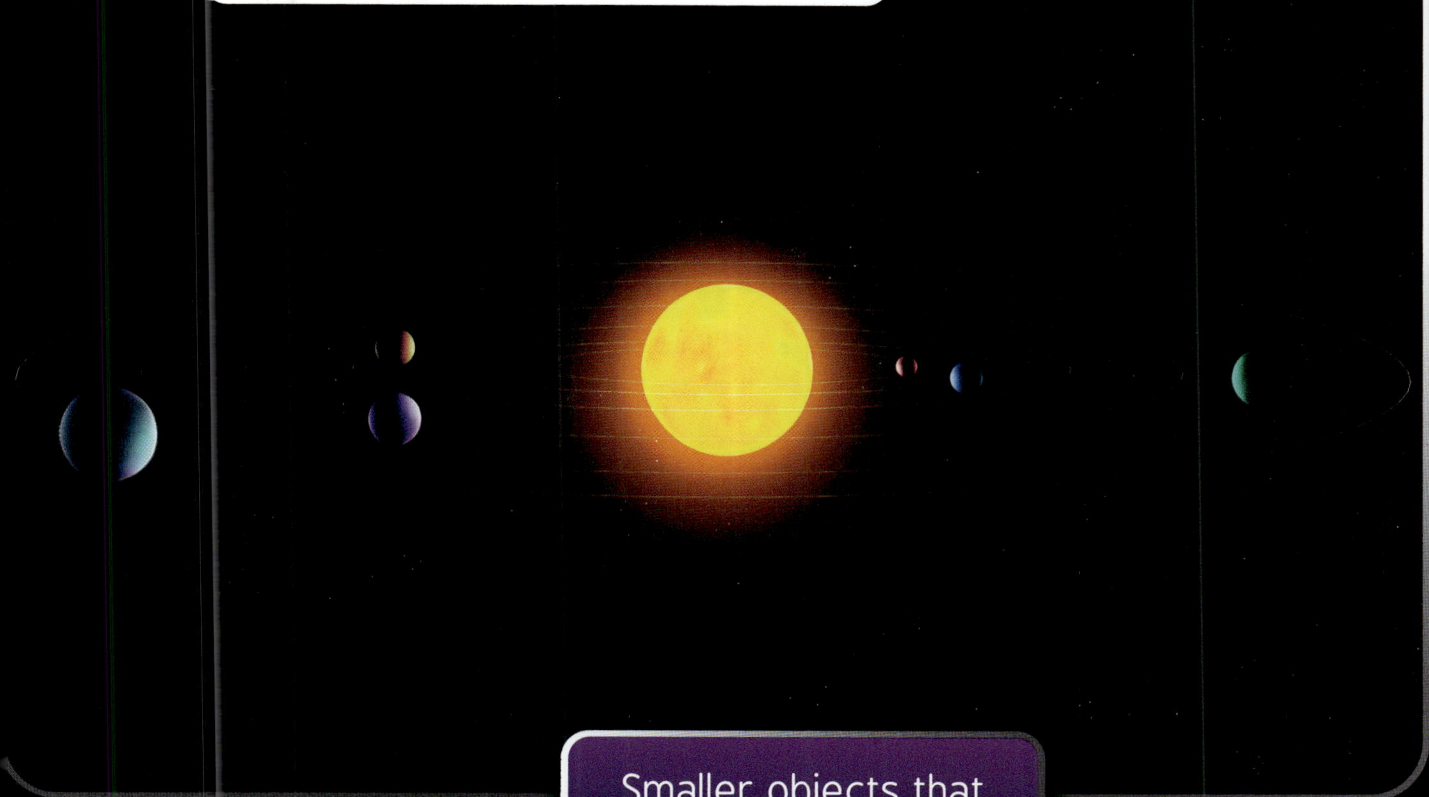

Smaller objects that orbit around planets are called satellites.

DWARF PLANETS

Dwarf planets are like regular planets in a lot of ways. However, they are much smaller. There are five dwarf planets in our solar system. The dwarf planets are called Ceres, Pluto, Haumea, Makemake, and Eris.

Scientists used to think of Pluto as a planet. However, it was later renamed as a dwarf planet. This was partly because it was not big enough and its gravity was not strong enough.

MOONS

A moon is something that orbits around a planet or a larger object that is not a star. Earth is not the only planet that has a moon. Many planets and dwarf planets have moons.

Moons are often made of rock.

Earth has one moon. However, the planet Jupiter has 95 moons. The solar system has over 290 moons in it that we know of. Venus and Mercury are the only known planets that do not have moons.

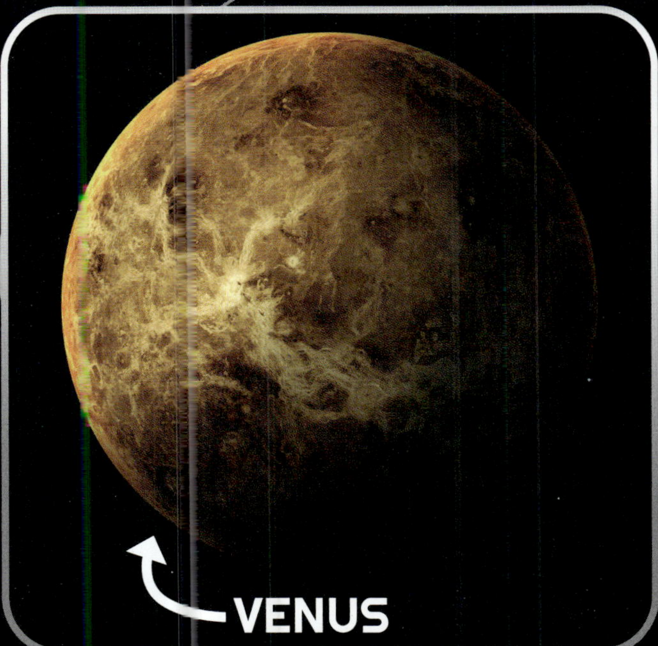

ASTEROIDS AND COMETS

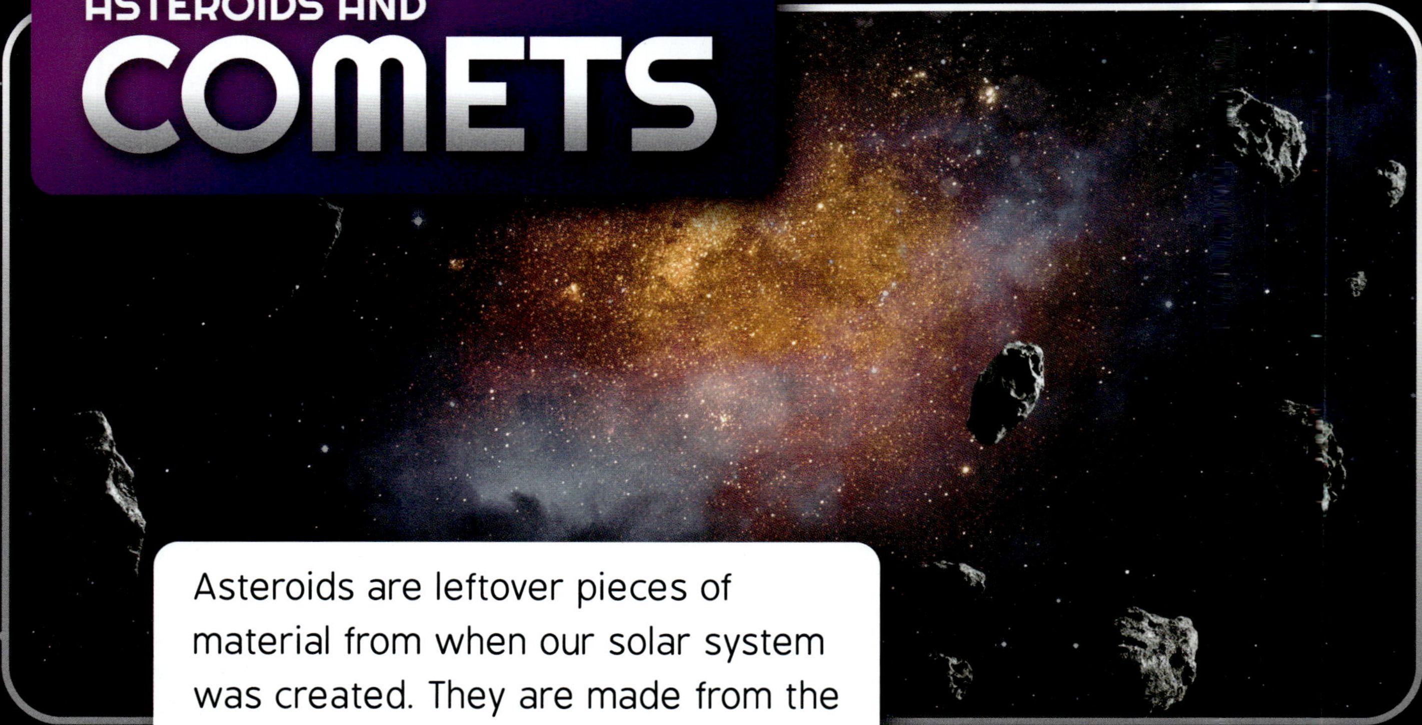

Asteroids are leftover pieces of material from when our solar system was created. They are made from the pieces of rock that did not become part of a planet, a moon, or the sun.

Shooting stars are smaller bits of asteroids that enter Earth's atmosphere.

Comets are balls of ice and rock. When comets orbit close to the sun, the ice heats up. This causes comets to leave trails of dust and gas that look like bright, glowing tails.

THE ASTEROID BELT

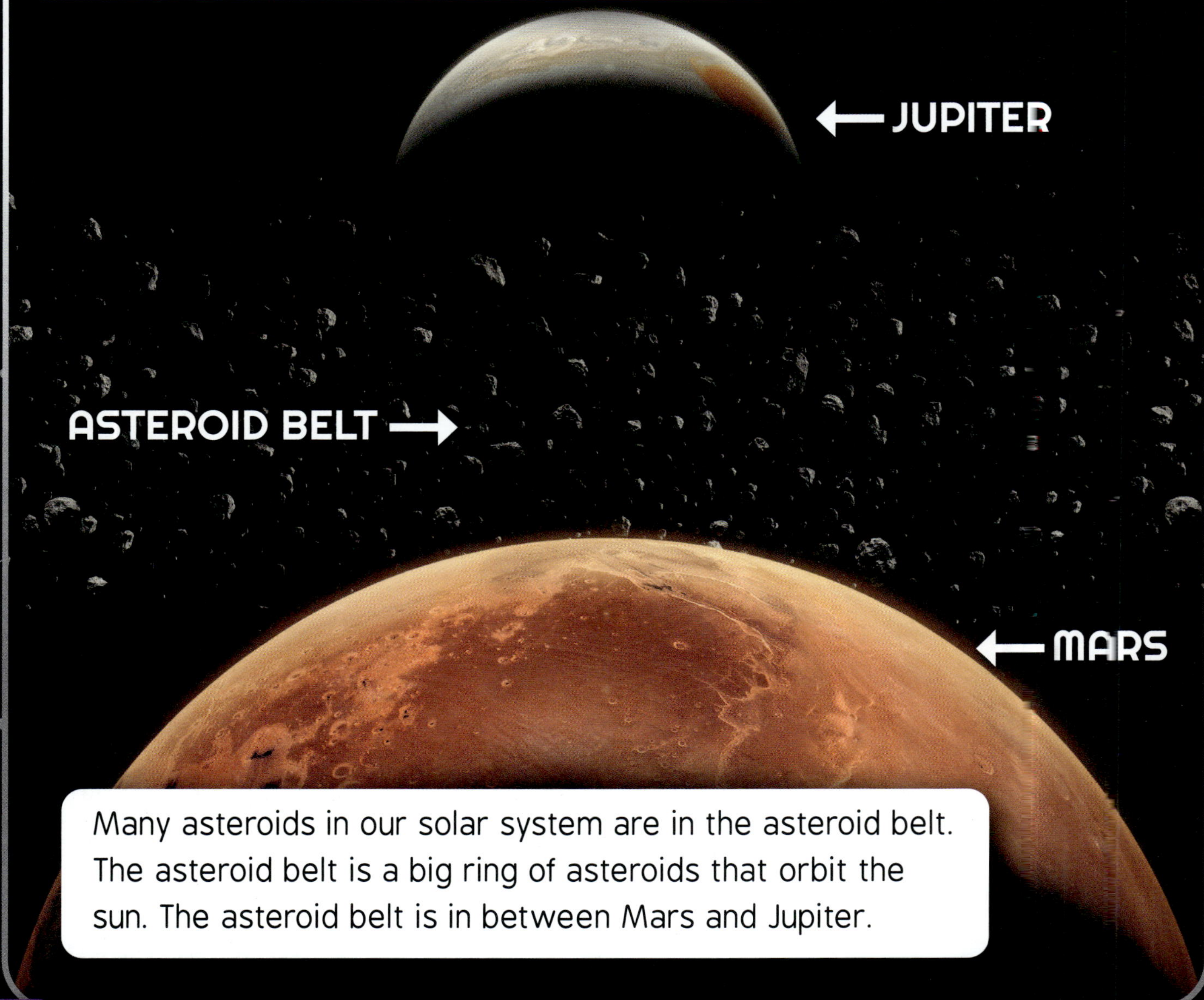

Many asteroids in our solar system are in the asteroid belt. The asteroid belt is a big ring of asteroids that orbit the sun. The asteroid belt is in between Mars and Jupiter.

The asteroid belt does not just have asteroids in it. Ceres, the dwarf planet, orbits inside the asteroid belt. Ceres is the largest object in the asteroid belt that we know of.

THE INTERNATIONAL SPACE STATION

In 1998, humans launched their very own space base. It is called the International Space Station. The space station is visited by astronauts from all over the world. They usually stay for around six months.

The International Space Station is a place where astronauts go to research space. Astronauts stay at the space station to discover different ways of staying safe and healthy while living in space.

At night, you can see the space station from Earth!

EXPLORING
SPACE

There is so much going on in the solar system. This can make it seem like a very big and busy place. However, our solar system is only a tiny part of space.

There are lots of other planets besides ours. Many scientists believe there are even more that have not been discovered yet. Do you think there are more planets waiting to be explored?

GLOSSARY

atmosphere the mixture of gases that make up the air and surround the Earth

gas a thing that is like air, which spreads out to fill any space available

gravity the force that pulls everything downward toward the center of large objects in space

orbit to move around a star or planet in a curved path

survive to stay alive

INDEX